The Network

Thomas Medonis

Fauci Aids Magic

Insurance

Death Row

King of Connecticut

Kneel?

ET

Food Wars

Treaty of 1213

Prince of Academi

FAUCI AIDS MAGIC

Thomas Medonis

I can't help but be quite speculative when I look back on the early 1990's era of Sports-Center and AIDS. It seems as if the two grew parallel in popularity. Why is that? I'll never forget November 7, 1991 when NBA Legend Magic Johnson announced his sudden retirement from the Lakers after testing positive for HIV. Shock spread throughout the world as a superhero contracted the "Gay Men's Disease". Sports media was now on top of the world at this moment in time. As "road culture" led to the encounter that infected Magic with HIV, he would take hold of the world "AIDS" stage.

For Magic to be the Spokesman for AIDS beginning in '91, he needed support. And playing in L.A. he found the greatest theatrical Health Director that ever walked the Earth- Dr. Anthony Fauci! A man that is listened to by masses, yet is proven clueless and colluding in every instant. Writer Larry Kramer claimed "40 million people (worldwide) who are predicted to be infected by the year 2000 are going to die", wherein fact less than a million have truly died of AIDS in the history of the United States.

AIDS Cure Unlikely in Time to Save Magic Johnson, Lee Siegel, November 11, 1991: "Magic Johnson, who calmly told the world he had the AIDS virus, now waits for the deadly disease to strike. There's faint hope researchers can find a cure or better treatment to save him in time. It may take several years before we develop a drug or combination of drugs that will have a substantial positive impact on the longevity of people who are now infected, said Dr. Anthony Fauci, who heads the federal government's AIDS research program. I believe we will reach that point, but will we be able to reach that point while Magic Johnson is still reasonably healthy? The answer is, I don't know. But we're making progress.... You should not take the attitude that Magic Johnson is a goner. Johnson could live five to 14 years, said Dr. Michael Gottlieb, who in 1981 wrote the first report on the disease now known as AIDS. He also treated actor Rock Hudson, whose death from AIDS brought the disease widespread attention… Critics say the government and drug companies are sluggish in seeking a cure. It's largely business decisions- profitability- and bureaucracy in the government drug-testing apparatus, as well as insensitivity by President Bush, Gottlieb said. Fauci defended Bush. When you look at what he's done, it's been substantial, he said. The federal government will spend nearly $4 billion on AIDS this fiscal year, including $1.5 billion for research, of which the National Institutes of Health got $852 million, Fauci said."

What if I told you that the more I dig and research, the more I conclude AIDS and Chronic Fatigue Syndrome (CFS) are one and the same. We have been blinded by our public servants and their manipulation of "Public Health". Fauci has been hated by the majority of the Gay Community since 1983. Why? Maybe, his deliberate ignorant fear mongering. Why has he never been pressed to answer real questions at his ten daily interviews? Was AIDS built in a lab by one of the original American bio-terrorist Bruce Ivins, who was funded by Fauci's institute. Bruce Ivins was a long-time bio-defense researcher at the U.S. Army's infectious disease research lab in Fort Detrick, Maryland.

There is no doubt that HIV was some type of experiment developed on the citizens of the world. Beginning November 22, 1991, Attorney General William Barr formed the world's first HIV detainment camp as the U.S. Government conducted universal HIV testing for all Haitian refugees at Guantanamo Bay who hoped to flee to America. Federal law, consequently, forbade the refugees entry into the United States with a failed HIV test. He held 310 Haitian Immigrants in HIV prison camps at Camp Bulkely on Guantanamo Bay.

"Their position was, 'Guantanamo is a military base, and why were all these people here, the HIV people, all these other people? How long are you going to be on our property with this unseemly business?" [Bill] Barr continued, "I'd say, 'until it's over. But we're not bringing these people into the United States.'" (Daily Beast, Scott Bixby, White House Reporter)

Clinton Administration Record on HIV/AIDS.

U.S. Department of Health and Human Services

"The Clinton Administration has responded aggressively to the significant threat posed by HIV/AIDS with increased attention to research, prevention, and treatment. Overall funding for AIDS-related programs within HHS has increased by 150 percent under the Clinton Administration, with funding for AIDS care under the HHS Health Resources and Services Administration's Ryan White CARE Act increasing by 358 percent and assistance for the purchase of AIDS drugs increasing by 965 percent. The FY 2001 budget includes $9.2 billion in total HIV/AIDS funding within HHS." (The Body, HIV/AIDS Resource)

Yes, it seems the promotion of increased funding was the priority, not public health, just as the Gay Community began to accept AIDS as cases increased.

"Disease Rumors Largely Unfounded", New York Native, May 18th, 1981, Dr. Lawrence Mass wrote, "Last week there were rumors that an exotic new disease had hit the gay community in New York. Here are the facts. From the New York City Department of Health, Dr. Steve Phillips explained that the rumors are for the most part unfounded. Each year, approximately 12 to 24 cases of infection with a protozoa-like organism, Pneumocystis carinii, are reported in the New York City area. The organism is not exotic; in fact, it's ubiquitous. But most of us have a natural or easily acquired immunity."

What if Chronic Fatigue Syndrome and AIDS are the same thing? (Fauci, Charles Ortleb)

Centers for Disease Control and Prevention: Emerging Infectious Diseases: Volume 5, Number 3- June 1999- Synopsis- Gabriella Campadelli-Fiume,

Prisco Mirandola, and Laura Menotti- University of Bologna, Bologna, Italy

Human Herpesvirus 6: An Emerging Pathogen

The Discovery of Human Herpesvirus (HHV-6)

Infections with human herpesvirus 6 (HHV-6)… is very common, approaching 100% in seroprevalence [the percentage of individuals in a population who have antibodies to an infectious agent]. Initially designated HBLV, for human B-lymphotrophic virus, HHV-6 was isolated fortuitously in 1986 from interleukin 2-stimulated peripheral blood mononuclear cells (PBMCs) of patients with AIDS or lymphoproliferative disorders. The PBMC cultures exhibited an unusual cytopathic effect characterized by enlarged balloon like cells. The causative agent was identified as a herpesvirus by electron microscopy and lack of cross-hybridization to a number of human herpesviruses. The GS strain in the prototype of the first isolates. Two additional isolates of lymphotropic human herpesviruses, U1102 and Bambian, genetically similar to HBLV, were obtained 1 year later from PBMCs of African AIDS patients. All of the isolates could grow in T cells (CEM, H9, Jurkat), in monocytes (HL60, U937), in glial cells (HED), as well as in B-cell lines (Raji, RAMOS, L4, WHPT). A new variant, Z29, subsequently shown to differ in restriction endonuclease pattern from GS-like strains, was isolated from PBMCs of patients with AIDS. The cells supporting virus growth were characterized as CD4+ T lymphocytes. The designation HHV-6 was proposed 1 year after discovery of the first isolate to comply with the rules established by the International Committee on Taxonomy of Viruses. More than 100 additional HHV-6 strains have been isolated from PBMCs of children with subitum or febrile syndromes, from cell-free saliva of healthy or HIV-infected patients, from PBMCs of patients with chronic fatigue syndrome (CFS), and from PBMCs of healthy adults- these PBMCs were cultivated for human herpesvirus 7 (HHV-7) isolation.

Is AIDS parallel to Chronic Fatigue Syndrome? Yes, through my recent research I conclude that Chronic Fatigue Syndrome is a result of HHV-6 just as it is a component within the AIDS Virus. HHV was discovered in AIDS patients. The HHV-6 public health problem was in part developed by Fauci too. Human herpesvirus 6 (HHV-6) is the unifying viral agent of 2 epidemics - AIDS + CFS, which should be considered one and the same. Multi-systemic problems of the HHV-6 spectrum include multiple sclerosis, fibromyalgia, autism, and even Morgellons. Yet, questioning his science in front of cameras would always become a threat to "public health".

Why do the most arrogant and dishonest scientific administrators have the most power?

Hypergammaglobulinemia, t-cell perturbations and persistent reactivated EBV and CMV infections- were the beginning of AIDS/CFS/HHV-6 disaster. A component of the immune system, a subset of T-cells called CD4 cells, were severely depleted. Findings would become prevalent of retrovirus particles in HIV-negative patients with AIDS-like symptoms. Apparently, Centers for Disease Control were already knowing of such HIV-negative cases of an AIDS-like illness. CDC scientists reported on six cases of non-HIV positive AIDS. Ironically, the HIV-negative AIDS-like cases were all Chronic Fatigue Syndrome sufferers. For years it was observed that some CFS patients met the government's defining criteria for AIDS on every count except infection with human immunodeficiency virus. (Osler's Web, Hillary Johnson)

Ironically, in the year 1984 the government certified HIV as the official AIDS virus. Thus with the idea in mind that "CFS is a covert form of AIDS", the sky was the limit.

"Life Unworthy of Life": Racial Phobia and Mass Murder in Hitler's Germany, Jame M. Glass wrote, "It was not cultural propagandists who organized the infamous 'special treatment' of the jews; it was the public health officials, the scientific journals, the physicians, the administrators, and the lawyers, who feared the very presence of the jews would endanger their families, their bodies, and ultimately their lives. To think of the jew in such terms is insane from our perspective, but it was held to be sane in the culture caught up in the phobic projection of infection onto the jews and the scientific authority legitimizing such beliefs.

AIDS Science could be described as Nazi Science, in that it is a continual development of an existing project that negatively harms the public, just as the Nazi Scientists were brought to America in Operation Paperclip in order to prolong all of their experiments. Thus the use of fraudulent and phobic public health concerns has created scapegoats and biomedical persecution of the unwilling or unwanted community. This is all still occurring in real time. Our science is not based on nature, it is now the study of abnormal theories, totalitarian demands, and sociopathic public servants, all concocted to raise vast capital.

Modern Science is no more than a "Scientific Ponzi scheme" (Fauci, Charles Ortleb). In 1980 the Bayh-Dole Act made it a law that scientists could get a portion of a patent from a vaccine they make for a company. Sponsored by senators, Birch Bay of Indiana and Bob Dole of Kansas, the 1980 Act was adopted and codified at 94 Stat. 3015, and in 35 U.S.C. 200-212, and is implemented by 37 C.F.R. 401 for federal funding agreements with contractors and 37 C.F.R. 404 for licensing of inventions owned by the federal government. More or less the Act's legislation controlled the inventions arising from federal government-funded research. Thus the government took over any type of scientific, intellectual, or industrial advancement.

Medical science would devolve as Fauci began work at the National Institute of Health (NIH) in 1968, and in 1977 he was clinical director of the National Institutes of Allergy and Infectious Diseases (NIAID). November 2, 1984 Anthony Fauci became Director of the National Institutes of Allergy and Infectious Diseases (NIAID). Through this position he would come to be known as the AIDS Czar.

Fauci saw AIDS as an opportunity for NIAID to develop great funds through a epidemic. He worked so hard for cutting-edge AIDS research and medicine, that he was rewarded with funds appropriated by Congress for AIDS research. Yet, Fauci still had to battle against the National Cancer Institute where "AIDS" was first discovered. Yes, AIDS involved Cancer, Kaposi Saroma, and Fauci still proved the necessity for the majority of funding for an "Infection Disease" and received ever evolving monetary quantities from the government.

Thus, Anthony Fauci, the business man, pushed to get the National Childhood Vaccine Injury Act (NCVIA) of 1986 passed that removed liability away from Pharmaceutical companies who had been sued for the Diphetheria, Tetanus, and Pertussis (DTaP) Vaccine injuries. Under the NCVIA, the Vaccine Injury Act was created to provide a federal no-fault system for compensating vaccine-related injuries or death by establishing a claim procedure involving the U.S. Court of Federal Claims and special masters. Fauci also pushed the AZT (Aidovudine [ZDV], also known as Azidothymidine [AZT]) "treatments for profit" on people with the AIDS virus. The AIDS treatment used to prevent mother-to-child spread during birth or after a needle stick injury kills healthy cells and doesn't cure AIDS.

In his book Good Intentions, Bruce Nussbaum writes, "In 1982, NIAID received $297,000 in AIDS funding. In 1986 it received $63 million. In 1987, the sum reached $146 million. By 1990, NIAID's annual AIDS funding was pushing half a billion dollars. Tony Fauci's ship had come in."

Sadly, the American Foundation for AIDS research (amfAR) played a significant role in funding HIV research and contracting celebrities into a 'shameful' HIV propaganda campaign. Just as in contemporary America, the American Foundation for AIDS private organization became an important propaganda machine for the government's HIV/AIDS establishment. The American Foundation for AIDS (amfAR) would censure and remove serious scientific criticism of the HIV hypothesis. Thus the entire scientific establishment working for the AIDS epidemic turned the entire world into a world of "heterosexist, totalitarian, and abnormal science."

Strangely, evidence of HIV wasn't found in all patients at the amfAR forum April 9th, 1988 at

George Washington University. The 'Scientific Forum on the Etiology of AIDS,' sponsored by the American Foundation for AIDS Research (amfAR), concluded HIV couldn't be the cause of AIDS. Yet, basically being gay, or later in AIDS development, black, was a pre-existing condition that led to the transmission of HIV. In his book Poison by Prescription, John Lauritsen writes on page 151, "The virus cannot be found in all cases of AIDS. On the other hand, "Fauci responded... by saying a good lab was able to isolate the virus in 90-100% of the cases... Fauci did not provide a reference to published data, nor did he indicate what the good labs were, or how exactly they differed from the to-so-good labs." (Poison by Prescription, p 151)

An editorial in <u>New York Native</u> read: "Last week Anthony Fauci of the National Institute of Allergy and Infectious Diseases asked that all cases of HIV-negative AIDS be reported to him. We reported thirteen million American cases. That's the estimate of the number of cases of Chronic Fatigue and Immune Dysfunction, a condition that research suggests is essentially HIV-negative AIDS.
(Osler's Web. p. 605)

The control of public health has sadly led to an arrogant, biased account of natural health. In reality, the public health establishment is actually a bought and paid for insurance and pharmaceutical Ponzi scheme. Subjective enterprise has become a slave to political manipulation. It is a closed-community of scientific experts.

Fauci wrote in the AAAS Observer on September 1, 1989, "When I first got involved in AIDS research, I was reluctant to deal with the press. I thought it was not dignified. But there was a lot of distortion by those who were speaking to the press so I changed my mind."

Independent journalism died at the outset of AIDS, there was a tragic relationship between big media and the 'sold-out' scientists. Fauci said in 1989, "the media are no place for amateurs, particularly when talking about a public health problem of the magnitude of AIDS." Fauci continued on, "Scientists need to get more sophisticated about expressing themselves. But the media have to do their homework. They have got to learn the issues and the background. And they should realize that their accuracy is noted by the scientific community. Journalists who make too many mistakes, who are sloppy, are going to find that their access to scientists may diminish."

PCB = Poison by Prescription: A 'Scientific Forum on the Etiology of AIDS, John Lauritsen

OW = Osler's Web: Inside the Labyrinth of Chronic Fatigue Syndrome Epidemic, Hillary Johnson

Insurance

Thomas Medonis

Many essays on the innate healing capabilities of the body in eastern and western medicine have been written. Yes, in my research in Taoism, Quigong, and meditation, eastern medicine prevails in certain health conditions, while western medicine, what I have experienced my whole life in New England, makes more sense in other instances. I always thought living in the state of Connecticut, known as the insurance capitol of the world, was an amazing feat in America. Geez, was I wrong with fantasizing about insurance. The power the insurance companies hold through the guise of liability is a nightmare for true natural freedoms. A feeling has always resonated within me that insurance was the biggest scam on Earth.

To understand the history of insurance as marine and fire insurance were the most prominent for centuries, one must understand the history of finance, otherwise known as the history of banking. Thus, it is a fair assessment to say health insurance is truly based on profit rather than health. And, through doctor and medical incentives the future medical prescription framework has distribution planned out for decades. What if risk insurance worked in the same promotional framework as health insurance?

Just as bankers, politicians, and hedge fund managers are able to pervade constitutional rights to access valuable information on private citizens and struggling business's, are investor's in insurance companies privy to the promotion of certain events or information?

Corporate insurance jurisdiction seems to take hold in America ironically in the same location I was born, Hartford, Connecticut. It was, however, earlier than my birth year of 1982 that a systematic juggernaut began to form, which would slowly defame any concept of free will.

The story of The Hartford Fire Insurance Company begins in 1810, when a group of a dozen investors formed a simple fire insurance company with working capital of $15,000. The very first President of Hartford Fire was Nathaniel Terry, who the group chose because of his standing as Mayor of Hartford and Congressman. It took only fifteen years of development to write the first insurance policy for Yale University. Yes, Hartford Fire started strong with shares valued as high as $100, yet, losses were incurred, premiums were wrongly priced, competition was fierce, and the American development of insurance was growing in complication. Some owners offered to sell shares for $5.

In 1835 the struggling company brought on a full reorganization. Eliphalet Terry, a minor investor, would become the president of The Hartford Fire Company and it is said, he took the small insurance company that insured a few warehouses in New York, and turned a New York tragedy into the transformation of the city of Hartford into the insurance capital of the world! Terry would thus insure all of the buildings that would consequently make up Wall Street.

Disaster in New York with the destruction of a huge fire in New York's financial district in 1835 led to a legendary trek Eliphalet would travel to calm, repay, and increase the insurance clients in New York under the policy of The Hartford Fire Company. Eliphalet Terry used his own private wealth to cover the reimbursement of all of the clients' claims for damage. He pledged his personal property at the bank in order that the insurance company's drafts would be honored. Terry, and company secretary, James Bolles, would thus travel 108 miles by horse drawn sleigh in the dangerous below-zero north-east winter to announce that the Hartford Insurance Company would pay for every claim in full!

The claims would total an estimated $20 million of property damage. The men would stay in New York for two months while paying claims, keeping confidence in customers, and selling a great amount of new insurance policies. Hartford Fire Company would consequently insure nearly every building to be rebuilt.

Through this great power grew many tragedies. Was it the hand of God? Or, was it the hand of man?

Notable tragedies:

New York City Fire, December 16, 1835, A gas line broke and the leaking gas then met a wood stove. A warehouse fire in the heart of Wall Street's financial district would spread block by block out of control, covering 17 city blocks and killing 2 people.

Chicago Fire, October 8-10, 1871, a "conflagration" (a large and destructive fire that threatens human life) began in a neighborhood in the southwest of the city after a long, hot, dry, windy period. It is written that the wooden construction led to the "conflagration" that destroyed over 3 square miles of the city, and killed 300 people. About 200 fire insurance companies worked in Chicago at the time, but the fire bankrupted 68 of them. Chicago policyholders recovered only about 40% of what they were owed.

San Francisco Earthquake and Fire, April 18-21, 1906, Hartford Insurance pays losses totaling $11.6 million. Fire caused through earthquake had some policies revisited.

Hartford Circus Fire, July 6th, 1944, Fire occurred during the afternoon performance of the Ringling Brothers and Barnum & Bailey Circus that killed 167 people. The fire started first as a small flame following the Lions' performance witnessed by Circus Bandleader Merle Evans. The cause of the fire remains unsolved to this day. Maybe, canvas sprayed with kerosene to prevent water from seeping in tent?

Is the hidden hand and insurance companies, one and the same?

Travelers Insurance developed the CAT Van in 1968, which was a specially modified RV used as a model claim office to assist policyholders after disasters. "Cat"astrophe Mobilization (Catastrophe Mobilization): Our dedicated Catastrophe Response Team and National Catastrophe Center coordinates response activity as a situation develops. In the event of a large catastrophe, we have thousands of employees available to help. (Travelers.com)

In 1995 The Hartford was acquired by ITT Corporation (worldwide manufacturing company based out of Stamford, CT) for $1.4 billion, which was the largest corporate takeover in American history at the time.

Death Row

Thomas Medonis

"I'm a dead man walking" - Tupac Shakur

Is the music industry the most corrupt of all media outlets? Is the music industry more so a money laundering outfit, rather a means of mind-altering entertainment? Have record labels been taking over by thieves, con-men, and radical police officers?

Why the small town of Compton?

The corrupt Compton Police Department was absorbed into the LA County Sheriff's Department instead of being eliminated completely.

Could Compton really be ground zero for the laundering of drug money into hip-hop music through many of the CIA's covert operations, such as "Operation New Wave"?

Maybe there is a reason many artists are not allowed to see the revenue based on their album sales or to know how much debt they accrued or how much profit they brought to the record label through concerts. Do artists really sell ten million albums?

Or, is the music industry a dark media outlet to maintain control over the populace.

    A great man by the name of Russell Poole will hopefully be known as a fighter for truth in our fabled American History. The former LAPD Detective's death will not lead us to forget about one of the few men inside the system trying to exploit the true nefarious nature of both the music and criminal justice systems. He had the courage to visit and interview the very people he suspected of wrong doing and, actually, requesting their help. "Strangely", Russell would die of a heart attack while attempting to provide a witness account at the L.A. County Sheriff's office in Monterey Park in the waiting room. Russell was asked to bring all of his case files saved on a disk when he reported to the Sheriff's office. He would report that a deputy had acted illegally and participated in Suge Knight's shooting.
 Ironically, the man to be silenced by the Sheriff's office, was the only true detective to solve the Tupac Shakur murder.

    Russell Poole believed that Los Angeles County Sheriff's deputies were involved with the shooting and cover up of Suge Knight in 2014. "The truth is that an off-duty Sheriff was videotaped letting the two shooters into the nightclub to kill Suge Knight… [And] the crime scene was purposely bungled by Sheriffs so that no prosecution could ever be made. The same off-duty Sheriff was caught on videotape dropping the shooters off at LAX" (Chaos Merchants: Murders of Tupac Shakur and Notorious Big, Michael Douglas Carlin and Russell Poole). Russell simply wanted to share his knowledge that an off-duty Sheriff had attempted the murder of Suge Knight. Suge Knight was no stranger to shootings as he was sitting next to Tupac as they were ambushed in their car. Detective Caffey DSD/CCAS determined that there were three separate hit contracts on Suge Knight's life.

Fox 11 Journalist Chris Blatchford received a confession letter to the murder of Tupac Shakur in 1998 from one of the shooters, who later was supposed to kill Suge Knight for the financial reward of a cashiers check for $100,000. A copy of the letter was given to Author Michael Douglas Carlin who published excerpts in Chaos Merchants, such as the excerpt: "A bounty was put on Tupac and Night." The shooter of Tupac is Lil ½ Dead (Chaos Merchants), whose motive for murder was based on being "Snoop Dog's" Cousin. Snoop had accumulated huge legal bill's for an acquittal in a murder trial, and "Death Row Records" through Suge Knight paid for the vast legal fees. Suge treated all his artists as his own children, even if they performed crimes. "He protects them, gets them legal help, bails them out" (Does a Sugar Bear Bite?, New York Times, Jan. 14. 1996). Thus, as Snoop's win in court was completely financed by his record label, Snoop would no longer be paid by Death Row for his new emerging hip hop music, all because of the accrued debt. Snoop couldn't receive any royalties until the legal fees from his murder trial were paid for (The Treacherous Two, Vibe Magazine, September 1998). Snoop would become frustrated with the lack of transparency within Death Row's Corporation.

It is written that these murder attempts are the result of the falling out between "Snoop Dog" and Suge Knight", amongst a much larger operation. Three days prior to the shooting of Tupac, an intense falling out occurred in New York, in which Snoop feared for his life flying back to the West Coast as his bodyguards were removed. "When I got on the plane to go to LA the next day, Suge didn't let none of my security ride with me. I had to ride on the plane with him, his homies, and Pac. And it was the most uncomfortable ride I had in my life" (Chaos Merchants).

The beef between Lil' ½ Dead and Tupac was much deeper as well, and was much more than an isolated shooting of Tupac in Las Vegas on September 7th, 1996. Lil' ½ felt Tupac stole one of his rap songs, and in fact, Lil ½ was beaten down by Tupac's bodyguards for disputing song's that were taken. "Jealousy" would be the shooter's justification for Tupac's murder. However, "if Snoop's cousin was the shooter in Las Vegas it is inconceivable that Snoop didn't know about [it] either before or after the fact" (Merchants of Chaos). The opportunity for the murder in Las Vegas of Tupac was "being controlled by" Reggie Wright Jr., head of Death Row Security and former Compton police officer, but most importantly Suge Knight's lifelong friend. Reggie Wright formed Wrightway Protective Services in May of 1995, wherein he would officially hire police officers through Wrightway while he oversaw security for Death Row Records. Wright would never let Suge out of his sight. "Reggie is the go-between, between Suge and all kinds of crazy" [stuff] (Russell Poole). "Reggie Wright Jr. was Suge Knight's biggest blind spot- his childhood friend- that could kill him and replace him" (Frank Alexander secret tape recordings of a conversation with Michael Moore).

"Mr. Writh Jr. gave info where 2 pac was going to be" (Tupac Shakur's murder Confession Letter received by Chris Blatchford on June 5, 1998).

The true intent of the 1996 Las Vegas shooting was also for the murder of Suge Knight, not just Tupac. A plot for murder was first conspired at Death Row Records in Los Angeles, and consequently, there was a "gang truce" meeting in Balboa Park to enable the gang hit against Tupac. Even considered Suge's blood brother, "Reggie Wright Jr. allegedly attended the gang summit and paid the $100,000 bounty to Danny Patton", where Wright asked for "direct permission to kill both Tupac Shakur and Suge Knight" (Chaos Merchants). Defined as a Blood and Crips truce meeting, the meeting was truly a means for Wright to see if Tupac's murder was a possibility as Wright wanted ownership to Tupac's material through Death Row Records, as well as the removal of Suge Knight. The American Entertainment Model: When you're worth more dead, the powers that be are going to put a bullet in your head! Furthermore, Lil ½ Dead didn't appreciate Suge Knight selling off his contract to Priority Records, and Suge didn't know Lil ½ Dead discovered the contract transaction, a move that made him leave Death Row; not that that knowledge would have changed anything. "So much of [Tupac's murder] had been executed just like a military operation" (Chaos Merchants).

Head of Death Row Security, Reggie Wright Jr., was also known to control the drug trade in Compton, as he would rob drugs and money from drug dealers instead of arresting them. This was before he discovered that gangster rap was a very lucrative business when on the Record Label's side. Thus, with the knowledge to plan crimes and compromise investigations, along with attorney David Kenner, Wright had the ability to erase the continual million dollar investigations by law enforcement agencies into Death Row's business. Consequently, according to many sources, Wright and Sharitha Knight, Suge's estranged wife, were the force behind the murder and murder attempt of all participants in Las Vegas September 7th, 1996. Sharitha Knight, even estranged, was the name on the paper next to Suge's name and all his assets. She was still privy to inherit all of his shares and assets. "Kevin Hackie claims he handed the weapon used in the Tupac killing to Reggie Wright two weeks before the killing" (Chaos Merchants). Suge Knight, adversely, was prevented by his attorney from discussing the shooting of Tupac on MTV a week after the shooting. He was blind as to Wright's true intentions. Why was the victim being silenced?

1st Degree Murder to promote capitalism now takes precedent in this nation. We live in a nation where friends and family hurt each other much worse than any enemy could. We were led to believe this was a battle of "west" vs. "east", bloods vs. crips, Biggy-Smalls vs. Tupac, but no, this is a much larger government-funded elaborative scheme to control information, drugs, money, and power. Something strange about Death Row Records was that from 1992-1996 Death Row earned $300 million in revenue, yet, "out of that, about $70 million in profit came back to the label" (Chaos Merchants). This is why every artist that left Death Row left broke and angry. Did they really sell all those albums?

Yes, there were rumors of money laundering, cocaine, and guns. Investigations by FBI, ATF, IRS, and police, which costs millions and millions of dollars for the taxpayer never led to any positive change or arrests, except for Suge Knight. His arrest quelled any further digging into Death Row. With such vast amounts of money, evidence, and manpower, how could nothing be found?

Well, to start, talent agents would passively work against the best interest of their clients in a passive aggressive manner. Suge and his crew, however, worked differently. They visited his accountant about 2 am with guns drawn requesting he tear up the records, as this was the time when the IRS started their investigation into Death Row. The record label was worth half-a-billion dollars. It is said the music industry is filled with crooks and that nobody gets proper bookkeeping, especially if all financial records are destroyed or manipulated. No one in Tupac's inner circle believed the rumors that "Puff Daddy" was responsible for the shooting of Tupac and Suge Knight in Las Vegas. Suge was not included in the planned shooting by Death Row employees because he was the target! Nothing can change the fact that of the $17 million Tupac was owed for his album "All Eyes On Me", nothing would be paid back to the Tupac estate as long as the true murder plot was concealed, which enabled the money to be laundered. When he died, Tupac was financially broke and only owned two cars, one of which was rewarded to him for appearing in a commercial. His music, hundreds of songs, however, will continue to be streamed for revenue all these years after his death. "During the period of his career with Death Row, Tupac never received an actual accounting from Death Row of the monies due to him. Instead, Tupac was repeatedly told by Knight, [attorney David] Kenner and other Death Row employees that he actually owed money to Death Row" (Afeni Shakur & Amaru Entertainment vs. Death Row Records February 12, 2008). Tupac put all the pieces together and realized that none of the Death Row artists will ever receive royalties shortly before his death. On the contrary, a government shut down of revenue for Tupac's music for a proper investigation of his death will never occur.

    Tupac's artistic value made his and Suge Knight's death very valuable occurrences. Here in America, we have lawyers who work for the BAR (British Accreditation Registrar) that will turn the most nefarious meditated crime into a celebrated holiday. "A good lawyer knows the law; a great lawyer knows the judge. But the best lawyers in Los Angeles Criminal Defense, including David Kenner, were part of the "Drug Club", an elite cartel of attorneys who handle all of the big cases and were wired into the system able to fix things that needed fixing" (Chaos Merchants).

    "[Tupac] had been on the set all day, and in the studio all night… He sent us to the studio to get cassettes of what he'd done the night before— he wanted to listen to it. They said no, that Kenner wouldn't allow it. Pac went crazy! He fired Kenner… I typed the letter… and he gave me permission to hire another lawyer" (The Takedown of Tupac, Connie Bruce, The New Yorker, July 7th, 1997)

David Kenner was known as a pay to play attorney, who worked for public servants that would return a reward for his services when his labor could not be afforded. As Death Row Record's attorney, Kenner represented Suge Knight, but he also represented Snoop and Tupac. Kenner would represent Snoop during his televised "Murder was the Case" real life trial. Just who would profit most with the elimination of two or the largest stake-holders in Death Row? At the time right before Tupac's death, Shakur was told of Kenner's conflict-of-interest and on August 27th Tupac Shakur fired David Kenner as his attorney. Kenner, also representing Snoop, began the rumor that Suge Killed Tupac.

Young talent growing up poor always follows the money. Prove me wrong.

That is how Death Row formed. Prior to the "The Chronics" album release by Dr. Dre, Dre and Suge, as two equal share-holders formed "Death Row" as a corporation. Waymond Anderson tells of "Suge Knight and Death Row Records actually laundering money for Michael and Lydia Harris instead of putting up the seed money"... Michael Harris had been convicted on drug charges establishing one of the largest drug trafficking rings in America. He had ties to many of the gangs that distributed his product" (Chaos Merchants). Waymond Anderson continued that Michael and Lydia Harris were also involved in an overthrow of Death Row at the time of the assassination of Tupac. The Harris's beef with Suge was due to the fact, "there was money that was laundered through death Row Records by Lydia while Michael Harris was in jail, and then they later came back and tried to say that they gave Suge money to start Death Row Records, which is totally untrue... But at the same time, when you grow up in inner cities the hard way, it's hard to walk away from the individuals you grow up with. So Suge still participated with individuals who were involved in criminal activity, and in doing so he laundered some money for Michael Harris, and then that later came back to bite him int the butt to where she and Michael felt that they should be provided profits from Death Row Records. And when Suge basically kicker her out, Michael and herself took that very personal, and from there it was on trying to get back at Suge Knight" (Waymond Anderson Deposition in the Wallace Civil Trial).

How is there any solution out there?

There were issues of off-duty police officers employed by Death Row Records, working alongside convicted criminals. "In fact, the off-duty police officers accompanied gang members during drug deals and acted as their lookouts and advisors. Moreover the off duty officers monitored police frequencies, assisted in choosing locations for drug transactions, and shared information regarding police tactics" (Wallace Civil Trial July 23, 2002 Order Granting and Denying Motions in Wallace Estate vs. City of Los Angeles).

"In May 1996, Death Row Records was investigated for zoning violations associated with numerous violent crimes. Investigating officers reported, 'There are armed security guards at this location in plain clothes and in security uniforms. These security officers are off-duty police officers ... employed by Death Row Records" (Wallace Civil

Trial July 23, 2002 Order Granting and Denying Motions in Wallace Estate vs. City of Los Angeles)

"On March 7, 1996, a fight occurred between Death Row Records personnel and Bad Boy Records personnel. Police officers responding to Death Row Records noted that [Snoop] was present at the location with additional members. Moreover, at least one off-duty LAPD officer, directly employed by "Snoop-Doggie Dog" as a bodyguard, was at the site" (Wallace Civil Trial July 23, 2002 Order Granting and Denying Motions in Wallace Estate vs. City of Los Angeles).

The murder of Tupac was the shining moment for the partnership of corporations, gangs and law enforcement. Tupac was getting billed by Death Row Records for $30,000 to $40,000 a month for security fees. "I think Tupac wanted to leave and Death Row didn't want him to go" (Michael Moore interview from Tupac Conspiracy, RJ Bond) Ironically, that same force he paid to protect him, executed the tactics behind his murder flawlessly. "There were spotters and radios. They selected a prime location on the edge of traffic" (Chaos Merchants). Security set-up like this will always continue all under the guise of another name, and another business, and another owner. Just as gangs and the mafia were used by rival business's, law enforcement personnel, who use their degrees, badges and guns to serve and protect the record labels that pay for their services, are also used to eliminate rivals. Suge said, "Well, look, we can't have our homies out here basically carrying guns, we want to legalize this. Let's set up our own Death Row security set under another name" (Kevin Hackie Interview with LAPD).

A great example of corruption in criminal justice was when "the evidence in Snoop's murder trial came up missing from an LAPD property room. That is why Snoop was acquitted" (Kevin Hackie Interview with LAPD). "At the party following Snoop's acquittal, Suge noticed that four of the jurors had shown up: They sipped champagne gorged themselves on steak and lobster, and mingled with the label's acts and associates. Tupac Shakur celebrated the fact that "All Eyez on Me" had debuted at No. 1. Suge told his lackeys he was renaming the company: From then on, it would be known as the New and Untouchable Death Row" (Have Gun Will Travel, Ronin Ro)

"On December 18, 1995, following the MTV Awards, Death Row Records members seeking Bad Boy Records' Combs reportedly assaulted an individual named Mark Anthony Bell. Two off-duty police officers were present during the assault of Mr. Bell" (Wallace Civil Trial July 23, 2002 Order Granting and Denying Motions in Wallace Estate vs. City of Los Angeles).

Interestingly, Sharitha Knight, as President of Knighlife Mangagement, was Snoop's manager from 1993 to 1996. What an intense time that must have been. Estranged Wife of Suge Knight was also dating LAPD Officer Kevin Gaines when Tupac was killed in Las Vegas 1996:

- Kevin Gaines had access to and was a suspect in the theft of evidence from an evidence locker being stored for the Snoop trial

- Gaines was on Special Assignment with other officers in Las Vegas the night of Tupac's assassination

- Gaines was shot and killed by Officer Frank Lygga. Lygga claimed the murder of Gaines was a sanctioned hit ordered by LAPD Police Chief Bernard Parks. "No it wasn't an accident."

- Gaines and Sharitha Knight were taken by Suge to a desolate desert location where he forced them naked and left them there to find their own way home. (Chaos Merchants)

"A Hampton, Virginia [concert] promoter has filed a $5000,000 lawsuit, plus punitive damages, against Snoop Doggy Dog, Sharitha Knight, and Death Row Records for allegedly duping her into trafficking drugs. Patricia Ann Richardson was arrested with seven pounds of marijuana on January 28, 1997. She claims that Mrs. Knight instructed her to deliver the packages to Snoop at a club and that she was not aware of their contents" (Vibe Magazine, February 1998).

How is all this possible?

How strong is the unification between law enforcement, organized crime, drug trafficking, human trafficking, arts and music?

King Of Connecticut

Thomas Medonis

As a starving artist I must say my best works have been when I was hungriest, angriest, or conversely, even most modest. Maybe my work sucks, but a majority of them have been best-sellers in their genre. I do give them all away for free through Amazon Deals and make maybe $5 a month off book sales. I obviously do not write to live, as I took to heart advice once shared from a patron who bought my book at the farmer's market, "Don't quit your day job."

At my age, a year from forty, I realize that to be a contracted author in with a big publishing house you must be compromised by the system. Just as the strange science fiction written in "Space Relations" and "A Planet In Arms" by Donald Barr may reflect. "Barr authored some strange fiction relating to adolescent sex slaves hanging out on another planet under the tutelage of a woman[.] [The woman] ends up arguably being a dead ringer for Ghislaine Maxwell… Maxwell remains under arrest after evading law enforcement for many months. Her credentials are also out of this world in that her father was a top Mossad spy who died under mysterious circumstances while many of her siblings have ties to the Jet Propulsion Laboratory in Pasadena, CA." (veteranstoday.com)

It is written that Ghislaine Maxwell's father, Robert, worked for Israeli Intel, British Intel, as well as for the KGB, as a multiple agent; codename: Little Czech. After Robert's death in 1991, possibly in connection to the Promis software scandal, his two sons' took over following the discovery that Robert had "misappropriated" monies from the Mirror Group's pension fund. Robert was broke at death.

Robert Maxwell's business dealings couldn't be salvaged and in 1992 Kevin Maxwell is known as claiming the largest bankruptcy in UK history with debts of 406.5 million pounds. The Maxwell's took part in the international war for the rights to the video game Tetris. Incredible legal battles erupted between Kevin Maxwell, Nintendo, and the Soviet State. The results would have a huge impact for the computer game publishing company Microsoft.

Conversely, sister, Christine Maxwell co-founded Magellan, one of the first internet content reference sites on the world wide web. Magellan was bought-out by competing search engine "Excite" in 1996 at a large profit for the initial investors. Christine Maxwell would also continue her working career in the publishing industry just like her father, as Robert built a publishing empire and greatly influenced the international games' software industry. She then re-invested and co-founded Chiliad, a data mining company, whose software supported data search technologies managed by the FBI's counterterrorism data warehouse.

Federal intelligence and law enforcement agencies have long used Chiliad's big data analytics platform to uncover information from a variety of data sources and platforms. Now the Herndon, Va.-based software company hopes to expand the reach of its data analysis tools to less technical users across a wider range of enterprises. (Chiliad Simplifies Big Data Search, Jeff Bertolucci, 10/8/2012)

"Chiliad makes use of on-demand, massively scalable, intelligent mining of structured and unstructured data through the use of natural language search technologies." (Gary Bello) Christine Maxwell also sat on the board of the Sante Fe Institue (SFI). As an independent, non-profit theoretical research institution, the SFI is dedicated to the "multidisciplinary study of the fundamental principles of complex adaptive systems, including physical, computational, biological, and social systems. Epstein openly donated $25,000 there in 2011... This one snippet shows a direct monetary link between Epstein and both Maxwell sisters at a time when Christine Maxwell was building databases that the FBI uses." (Jeff Epstein, the Maxwell Sisters and the FBI's Counter-Terrorism Database, Gerry Bello, Mockingbirdpaper.com)

Covert Intelligence operations and blackmail operations are nothing new to maintain the status-quo of arrested development. In the late thirties, Meyer Lansky, known as the "Mob's Accountant" would develop the National Crime Syndicate (NCS). Associated with the International Jewish Mafia, the NCS would send mistresses of the mob to Mexico, and other North American destinations, to try and lure diplomats and "bug" departments for blackmail material. Not long after these operations, Lansky became a covert agent with the OSS (Office of Strategic Services) during World War II.

The OSS and NCS alliance was said to be formed out of war-time necessity and was defined as "Operation Underworld". Following the war, however, the alliance continue on. "It continued to grow and really proliferated, especially after the 1960s when the CIA hired several Lansky associates for assassination teams" (The Jeffrey Epstein Scandal Is Much Bigger Than Jeffrey Epstein, August 15, 2019, truthdig.com)

    Was the true purpose of Donald Barr's literature connected to his position as Office of Strategic Services (OSS) Agent, administrator at Columbia University, or former Headmaster at Dalton School (Alums include Anderson Cooper)?

> The [Dalton] [S]chool, which had been a progressive haven for the children of artists and writers, was undergoing a shift under a new headmaster. Donald Barr, the father of Attorney General William Barr, came in as a disciplinarian focused on beefing up the academics of the school, and on enforcing a strict code of conduct… If Mr. Barr caught students using marijuana, he would often send them to therapy as a condition of staying in the school… In February 1974, Mr. Barr had announced that he was resigning as headmaster, protesting the meddling by the board of trustees, but that he would stay on until the end of the school year. It is unclear whether Mr. Barr hired Mr. Epstein during that time. Mr. Epstein, from Brooklyn, was just 21 when he joined the faculty at Dalton, arriving without a college degree. The school's student newspaper reported in September

1974 that he was starting that year as a math and physics teacher. (New York Times: Jeffrey Epstein Taught at Daulton. His Behavior Was Noticed. Mike Baker and Amy Julia Harris July 12, 2019).

Everything I write goes against the mainstream systems ideology. Spirit is sanitized by the mainstream, while the spirit drives me. There is a moment right now that never existed before. Two separate magnificent worlds facing off. The synthesized man-made masterpiece or the natural creative grafting harmony of God's Universe. On the former side, pump vaccines and munch on gigantic produce dependent on blue fertilizer, or the latter, find your medicine in organic food. Sadly, a natural plant that I attribute my success and survival in this concrete jungle too is now being high-jacked. I got my medical ganja card in Connecticut as soon as I could get it. In sharing all my personal history with a wonderful physician, he would learn all the things that would change a child to hold a different energy, something I would prefer to only share in my literature and with my doctor. I thought having the card would lead to growing my own organic herb, something I've never seen available. How is this fair at all. I am certified organic and can't even grow my own medicine! The "State" of Connecticut once again has no interest in my own or the entire public's health and well-being.

So frustrated on so many levels with our governing bodies, only to discover, my physician was charged somewhere around $20,000 to have all of his records audited recently. This just really deflated any hope I had in our State's respect for the privacy of medical history or the correct management of marijuana by a bureaucratic monster. Unfortunately, I never think of the political aspect in why things are the way they are, but I really can't but only say everything in Connecticut is make believe "State Sponsored" advertising. With the State's infiltration into everyone's records who do not go to regular doctors because they realize their life would be in harm because of the insurance system's value on deceased talented individuals, Weed is legal in Connecticut July 1st, 2021. I just read today that Governor Ned Lamont's wife, Annie Lamont's, finance company is officially the only company you can get financed through for a grow lab in Connecticut!

This system is just so blatantly one-sided for those compromised to perform. Where did Governor Lamont get his systemic know-how from? Well, his father Edward Lamont was a JP Morgan banker and Chairman of the Children's Aid Society. "After graduation from Phillips Exeter and Harvard, Lamont started his career developing aid programs under the Marshall Plan and later joining the World Bank. He worked in International finance at JP Morgan, back to Washington as a director at HUD, and back to New York as President of the Morgan Community Development Corp., which financed low and moderate income housing. He authored several books, including "The Ambassador from Wall Street", and "The Forty Years that Created America", a new perspective on the very different histories and motivations behind our earliest settlements- Plymouth and Jamestown. (New York Times, Paid Notice: Deaths Lamont, Edward M).

Stealing ideas and stealing the natural remedies provided by God are not cool. I just wish not to think of the web of espionage and how it effects each and every one of us. Is there a systemic group of nefarious actors led by intelligence networks that tirelessly labor to find the next billion dollar "Golden Governor"?

What do we the people do when we are run by a tyrant, who uses non-violent legislature to make his family become billionaires. Is King Ned related to the Right Honourable Lord Norman Lamont of Lerwick, the Pilgrims Society Member. And, the Pilgrims Society is rumored to be the most dangerous secret society in the world! During the 1933 World Economic conference attended by 66 nations, in the summer of 1933, held at the Geological Museum in London, a Pilgrims Society farce would play out, only benefitting the banking powers with the great result of grief and poverty for the rest of the world. As it is written, the Pilgrims Society is the alliance of US & UK elitism dating back to 1902.

"The Pilgrims Society London [also] ping-ponged silver across the Atlantic Ocean over to The Pilgrims Society USA to take over the silver conspiracy. The real goal of the [Silver Purchase] Act (June 1934) was to concentrate history's biggest silver stockpile in the Treasury Department so the financiers would have a supply of silver with which to manage world silver prices for several generations into the future." (nosilvernationalization.org)

Lord Lamont, at the center of British politics for many years, was too a longtime director of N.M. Rothschild. The British multinational investment banking company controlled by the Rothschild family first employed Norman in 1968, and he would be come to known for working with super high net-worth individuals. Furthermore, Norman would hold the chair for the G7 Finance Ministers and hold "Chancellor of the Exchequer" (finance Minister) from 1990-1993. He also chaired the British-Iranian Chamber of Commerce! Lord Lamont would also serve as an advisor to Monsanto, which was also one tentacle of world history's most evil secret society.

Lord Norman Stewart Hughson Lamont was also chairman of Le Cercle, a secretive elite foreign policy club, that met bi-annually in Washington, D.C. Le Cercle's Parliamentary Private Secretary committed suicide less than a month after the ELM GUEST HOUSE boy brothel was raided. UK army intelligence officer was jailed after disclosing that the British Intel Agency MI-5 was organizing child abuse at the Kincora Boys home in order to control top people.

When will this mayhem of creating a satanic reality based on designed child abuse operations stop? I always say, "to find the solution we must go back to the beginning." Well then, I sure do know where to start looking for solutions! The Connecticut Charter is the most important document to ever be published and signed by a monarch of the United Kingdom. "Governor John Winthrop of Connecticut, received the great news on May 10th, 1662, that the King [Charles II] finally granted the Charter.

According to the Charter, Connecticut Colony included parts of New York, Pennsylvania, Ohio, Indiana, Illinois, Iowa, Nebraska, Wyoming, Utah, Nevada, and California. Cotton Mather called the document, "The freest Charter under the cope of Heaven." (The Charter, Thomas Medonis)

Kneel?

Thomas Medonis

The minimal labor to create this Short-Read is to help get the word out there about the brilliant lifetime of a man, whose understanding of grammar and its impact on global affairs has completely disabled the New World Order's effort for global dominion. An American Hero, who withstood numerous beat downs because he didn't use the elite legislatures and judiciaries 'adverse' grammar, is known as Russell-Jay: Gould. Somehow, the "now time", has been overlooked in all basic bookkeeping and banking. The construct of an "independent jurisdiction" was a whole new system of mathematical and logistical grammar. Gould would reassess all masonic books that establish crown authorization, and in doing so, formed a federal government system based on quantum truth in contract and deed. Simply, it was mathematically certifiable grammar. Validation could be made on timelines forwards and backwards.

1988, April 6, Russell-Jay: Gould's partner David-Wynn broke the Mathematical interface on grammar. "I proved that all grammar, all languages are a mathematical equation of algebra… Rewrite the way grammar is used." (David-Wynn: Miller)

Miller focused on mathematical relations in grammar. Gould, however, investigated mechanics on a global level: banking, postal, military, court mechanics. Gould's curiosity parallels why I write- why things are the way they are?

Even as a very important world citizen, arrested and beaten, Russell had a system of weights and measures in coordination with strategic metals contracts which gave him authorization to print and mint our own countries coinage for the first time ever! Gould also built in 2003 the quantum banking construct, which had the ability to translate all world language to make international trade and banking fair to all nations. Everything has been saved for the good of the people by this man's efforts on a global scale. Russell-Jay: Gould's new concept for citizens to "Claim of Life" is the first step to claim oneself a sovereign and to rid our dependence on the birth certificate system that truly ended in 1999. Gould also created the quantum banking system for about everything on earth- 82 treaties with different countries on earth. Ironically, Gould's solutions were to be found in America's biggest financial demise, even though it was most likely all planned out by those that rule the Republic of America.

To understand why Gould is so important, we must understand International Bankruptcy Law.

International Bankruptcy, how long does it last? 70 years.

The third and final Bankruptcy for America began on October 29th, 1929. 70 years later on October 12, 1999 Gould filed copyrights on the Title 4, U.S.C. 1, American Flag. Gould provided the definitive quantum grammar on how the flag would be filed with United Nations and international postal service unions, as the US post office authorizes outside country's governments worldwide.

The old masonic system of shipping wars, banking wars, insurance wars, oil wars, are all based in admiralty and maritime law. Birth certificates are a commercial instrument that claims us as cargo, subject to laws of The State. We have been set up to be no more than a global financial system slave. Children are given social security numbers, which estimates how many taxes they will pay their entire life, and these figures are manipulated and waged on through Wall Street. In the courts, we are viewed as property who lost rights through the submission of our birth certificate.

Great Britain's King held control of the American Corporation up until 1999, all because he was the world's post-master general. King of Great Britain is ruler of the "vessel" or the "post" we all inhabit. He is the reigning monarch of the world. We are all on his boat, as the system is so easily non-violently enforced in the courts. Contracts within the system are enforced in neutral courts, which are the new frontier of war upon the sovereign world citizen. They always win, thats the set-up. You are no more than a valuable piece of cargo for pirates. The system is defended by the King of Great Britain, post master general of the world, who will do any deed to continue dominion. Acts performed through the Masonic system controls all facets of the entire system. We are fed propaganda and we must love it! Furthermore, the media is owned by the system of control, who promote artificial crisis to enhance wealth, as the King of Great Britain's contracts are all interpreted the same by all countries. Yes, each country may hold a strategic metal contract, but it is the high ranking masons in each locality that authorize the minting of metals based on the individual banking system.

Think of our two party system: Republicans and Democrats. What if the purpose of the two, if Rhinos' were absent, was that the Republicans were for the Republic and the Democrats were for socialized democracy as practiced in Great Britain under their King. In America, the Crown derives authorization because there are very few true Republican legislators.

Complete shock fills my mind when I think that the construct of a copyright contract and patent for the American flag are what saved the Republic. Terms of the flag in bankruptcy ended in 1999, as the copyright on the flag in terms of grammar. Gould realized this and hustled to provide a "now space" American Flag for terms of contract. Contracts would thus perform in alliance with grammar at a quantum level. Gould first spoke to the United Nations and asked if they had a patent and copyright for the Title Four American Flag. Either way, any contract was in grammatical error. Gould rewrote the copyright and patent for the Title Four American Flag so it wasn't surrendered back to Great Britain. Through his discovery to the UN, Gould is distinguished as a sovereign.   He disqualified the entire old system.

A bankruptcy trust was no more or no less what the constitution accomplished in 1789. The first of three 70 year bankruptcy's was for 3 million dollars in 1789. The Bank of England through the Rothschild family held the notes. Furthermore, the Constitution was written in parse grammar, which left words bastardized, as nouns, verbs, adjectives, etc, would mean the opposite of what they present. Terms of a tribe in ancient times were found under hieroglyphics or a flag, not in the opinion of the news media or legislature.

Unfortunately, with the confusion in who the bearer and owner of the American flag are following the final American bankruptcy ending in 1999, the post office is no longer eligible to log registration for the military. The US Postal service lost authorization because it lost its flag, it had no authorization to register anyone to join the military. Fraud was performed by the postal service by entering recruits into the military. Why is there no transparency in the correct grammatical governmental position? There is no accountability for the corruption. Contracts are manipulated under false terms. Business is regulated under law of a foreign flag.

On February 20, 2003 a peace treaty was authorized by the Secretary of the Navy under the

Title 4 American Flag. Secretary of the Navy signed peace treaty terms. However, the treaty was breached when the government used brute force to remove Gould from the Pentagon. The largest court martial in the history of the world, 2004-2008, would then proceed through the violation of contract. Everything since 1999 by our government has been done under false pretense, there is no president, there is no post office.

December 12, 2004, America was under martial law. Our public servants are truly at war with their people, but the people don't know it. Martial Law guidelines are filed under war powers claims- US SOCOM. All laws, all senate, all contracts, and all representation is closed for business under Martial Law. Strangely, the US judiciary is flying the yellow border fringe flags, which present a violation due to the addition of things onto the flag. The flag is a foreign fiction, just as our military, courts, and judges. All judges now solely act in a fictional setting - actors on a stage. Thus, this is the true nefarious business of harvesting people's assets and souls; it the the sole role of the current courts.

Thus, there are two different interpretations of our defined American Flag. One interpretations leads us to continue blind faith in a bankrupt system. The other interpretation, the law of the flag, expresses that the bearer of the flag is now controlled by Russell-Jay: Gould. A move that forces federal contractors to go through Gould to move goods and make contracts. He would also set up the charter for the universal postal union, which disabled the United Nations contractual universal postal system with each abiding country. Gould would tirelessly labor to reconstruct charters nation to nation, as he had the capacity to set up a countries own shares and share holders. The quantum banking system through Gould reevaluated the entire global monetary blueprint. Precious metals were brought into the quantum banking system, when prior, there were no credentials for guidelines as the American Banking System had no flag. Quantum banking helps people in terms of a more defined knowledge of how money is spent. A fair passing of goods, along with equity for equity, is the system that needed to be installed following America's final bankruptcy.

      Through Gould, and his partner Miller, grammar was used to advocate modification. Manipulation of the rules on the formation of grammatical sentences has been performed for time immemorial. Control of the language within the Bible was sought by the most high and powerful, as grammar is in control of concepts in the bible. Sadly, those most powerful rulers always make the choice not to be correct and truthful. The most high on Earth doesn't use fact, and that is why we are stuck in this hidden Masonic nightmare. Quantum banking aligned with Constitutional grammar has the power to stop continued war based on false pretense declared by actors. However, as long as the force against the people finds strength through religion and covert military actions we are in big trouble. Terms of the performance must always be known, no more special operations against anyone. Weed out corruption. Accountability brings about solutions. We must again hold value in an honor system based on truth and contract alignment

    Gould did it. He had the courage. No fear stopped him from creating the federal contract for the terms of the agreement with the existing contract for the Title 4 American Flag. He made sure to have correct grammar within the construct of the patent and copyright. Quantum language for United Nations voted to have an independent country to have an independent flag. All treaties were put in place for quantum computing and the process of quantum banking took off.

The title 4- section 1,2, 3, American Flag use lawsuit on July 25, 1999, challenged the correct sentence structure of the copyright of the "true" flag of America. Senate, Legislatures, Congress, and Supreme Court, had no comparable standing for the American Flag. On the 12th of August, 1999, the United Nations declared both men, Gould and Miller, as independent sovereign individuals. Not only did they 'capture the flag', but they also established treaties with other countries. They had the ability to withdraw money from their own bank, and read their own constitution.

If it weren't for Gould the 1999 Government Reformation Act would be the only governing mechanism to date, even though it does still seem to prevail. The UN plans would be fulfilled as a UN de-facto one world government would develop the globe how they saw fit. All banks would have to come under one banking system. For example, the wars in the Middle East true purpose was to steal oil and collapse the middle eastern independent banks. Terrorism is a fraud. The enemy is whoever doesn't go along with their new world order soap opera. Manufactured crisis, permanent war, permanent poverty, and permanent debt are what the powerful crave.

In 1999, on August 12th, Gould and Miller rewrote the construct, but had to wait later into 1999 when the US Constitution was no longer a source for guidelines due to international bankruptcy laws. Gould, consequently, had to file the contract with the post office in Washington D.C. Finally on November 2nd, 1999, the US post office in Washington D.C. was open for capture for eighteen days with the end of our third international bankrupcty. During this eighteen day period, America was vacated by the crown's reign, wherein the United States couldn't perform international trade and commerce. The 'Amero', a hypothetical common currency that would replace other foreign currency, was set up as the next American-European dollar. Gould, fortunately, during the eighteen day bankruptcy closure, took command and control of the post office as the new "Post Master General" for the world. It doesn't appear this way, but Gould truly ended the efforts of the King of England to reclaim America as a corporate entity.

Gould knew that terms of the flag in contract law were what made the document legitimate, and controlled the grammar of the federal contract style. The 3rd strike rule, with 3 strikes and your out, is a rule in international bankruptcy law based on a 70 year moratorium bankruptcy . With the third and final strike, the crown steps in, pays the debt, captures the flag, and the system. 1999 was supposed to be the year America surrendered to Great Britain for another extended bankruptcy period or even worse. Guidelines for the presidency in 1999 were to be vacated as well as the post service and post office. No founding fathers are alive to sign off on an amendment or correction to change the terms of the constitution for three continuous bankruptcies.

The brilliant Gould knew there would be no President elected in 2000. There should have been no presidential election in 2000 as we were bankrupt and were following no guidelines for government. The CHAD "punch-hole" ruse in Florida 2000 was no more than an excuse to obtain the ability to elect a president into the hands of the Supreme Court. The Federal Government vacated its guidelines for president through the Florida Chads. The continual operations and functioning of a president at all times was violated because no guidelines to elect an American President was prescribed; every election since is null and void

The punctured chad was no more than a great ruse, so the American People can easily be captured in usury compliance through the CIA- 5-star trust. The CIA has funded covert drug running operations for years and years inside America through this 5 star trust, along with many other nefarious operations. Incredible amounts of money were brought into the trust through foreign narcotics to fund covert operations against Americans. Grammar was completely manipulated and words did not match the intelligence agency's actions. Instead of honestly telling the American citizens that we are bankrupt in 1999 and don't have the standing to elect a president in 2000, the federal government in coordination with the Supreme Court fraudulently elected George Bush based on CHAD's.

Consequently, more dark money will be obtained through the United Nations institution of the global tax on every global citizen through the sustainability development fund, which currently funds black ops and the shadow government bank account. How much bigger will the sustainability budget get if the entire world pays into it?

What intuition! Gould filed contract with the postal service, and mailed the document to postal headquarters in Washington D.C., using proper grammar every instance. Ironically, through identification and timing, Gould would somehow become post master general by a signature over a postal label- otherwise defined as a ticket or postage stamp. The signature affirmed he was post master general by contract.

We'd be in big trouble without Gould's foresight, as the courts have become based only on opinion not fact. Facts are no longer the most important source for evidence in the court. Only condition of mind matters now during trial. But Gould knew about 1999, the end of America's third and final bankruptcy, and he built the construct of the constitution and bill of rights contracts. Thinking will always change, but facts can be documented and formulated in a manner that aligns with our founding principles. Gould discovered this and allowed us simple folk to deal as sovereigns in the modern world of constitutional claims and rights.

What flag or charter does our current President rise or kneel for?

E.T.

Thomas Medonis

Perhaps the most familiar example of mistaken sense-reports is that of the movement of the earth. The senses of every person report to him that the earth is a fixed, immovable body, and that the sun, moon, planets, and stars move around the earth every twenty-four hours. It is only when one accepts the reports of the reasoning faculties, that he knows that the earth not only whirls around on its axis every twenty-four hours, but that it circles around the sun every three hundred and sixty-five days; and that even the sun itself, carrying with it the earth and the other planets, really moves along in space, moving toward or around some unknown point far distant from it. If there is any one particular report of the senses which would seem to be beyond doubt or question, it certainly would be this elementary sense report of the fixedness of the earth beneath our feet, and the movements of the heavenly bodies around it—and yet we know that this is merely an illusion, and that the facts of the case are totally different. Again, how few persons really realize that the eye perceives things up-side-

down, and that the mind only gradually acquires the trick of adjusting the impression?

Clairvoyance And Occult Powers, Swami Panchadasi, 1916, p. 13

Here on Earth, if you don't program your mind, it will be programmed for you. If the sole intention is to judge we will learn nothing. Think of your soul's development just as the growth of a flower, this idea will begin the soul's attachment to the correct cosmic ideals. Idea's become ideals! Why not align yourself with the greatest natural forces that have survived millions of years within the universe. Feeling's that cultivate the soul's development are just as necessary for spiritual growth, just as the water, nitrogen, and calcium are for the plant's development. For a plant to grow it depends on the rays of the sun as well. True natural growth comes through ascension toward unification with the finer elemental forces. Just as hearing good music makes you want to dance, the sun rays makes the plants want to move in a positive way. The way the infant plant hears and feels the rays, and develops and blooms into a vibrant fragrant energy, is how our soul must listen and hear the supersensible forces that constitute spirit. Spirit has no confines within time and space!

To perceive and discover the lines, figures, and functions found within spiritual vision, we must surrender our feelings for material objects in order for the spiritual world to open up for our soul. As our soul is a flame that is veiled from optical vision because of slumbering functions; our organs, our brain, and our heart are all not reaching their divine potential. Envision the soul as a miniscule seed that receives the great forces of the universe that develops that seed into a giant flowering tree- growing, blooming, flourishing. There is no end in sight for the soul's development unless the wrong forces are being fed to the soul. The sunrise represents growth, while the moonrise represents decaying. We can sit in stillness and realize our mind, soul and physical body are all related to the minerals, plants, and animals that inhabit the Earth to form man and women- the ultimate observatory sign of the souls great powers. Incorporation of the relations of the living beings with the cycles of the universe within us will reveal the spiritual life force!

Unfortunately, in these difficult days our energy is all fed into illusion. We get so mad, fearful, and sad, at the media propagation, that we have no time to identify with the spirit. The force that can't be recorded has no time or space, and some consider these invisible universal energies as "Occult Forces". A great test to see where your soul's spiritual development is would be to listen to contrary views to your ideology. Do you get fired up? Or, do you have the ability to silence your intellect? In speaking with someone who you feel is far beneath you, do you suppress your superiority, or do you share your ego?

It is true that we can't see with our eyes the spiritual reality present in all living beings, but, too, we must not confuse our imagination with spiritual forces. The internal process of the seed is what we must understand, as well as obtain the ability to recognize the subtleties of the perceptive spiritual sound that forms nature's harmony. Even as soul and spiritual powers are subtle and indefinable, sound serves as a medium between individual soul and the spirit world. Our whole physical, etheric, and mental bodies must unite to form one unit serving as the spiritual ear and eye to become one with the spiritual impulses and colors. The boundary between the inner physical world and the outer body world must permeate into one. This is the link for human development to advance toward cosmic adaptation. The supersensible forces that control our very thoughts are what truly affect our sensitivities and desires.

Independence from the physical body is a good starting point for spiritual awareness. The ability to mentally vision your own self outside of your self is imperative for soul perception. If you are unable to first recognize your own bodily impulses, you will not recognize any outside of your body. To encounter the soul's perception makes one independent of the physical body, as our soul's jurisdiction is within the spiritual realm. And consequently, development of the soul comes through the pure thoughts of the living spiritual forces. When the dust of our soul no longer needs the physical body, we are home.

But yes, there are "Guardians of the Threshold" *(Knowledge of the Higher Worlds and Its Attainment, Rudolf Steiner)* that keep us from reaching home again. Superstitions, religions, dreams, all retard the psycho spiritual inner experience because all of those thoughts are outwardly perceived. And, if you are fortunate to overcome the "Boogey Man" of your greatest fears at the threshold of the spiritual realm, a luminous being will be awaiting for you as you surpassed the great deception. The senses are what have allowed for this great trickery, but truly the senses and the sensible are all recognized as a result of the supersensible forces. Thus, the ability to feel every impulse, vibration and color will all collectively bloom into a perfect union of spiritual forces. Thoughts are simply supersensible spiritual substance, also considered as spiritual dust. And this supersensible region outside the physical body is the new frontier for the developing human being. With no measure of time or space, can the soul survive such conditions? Will great appetites and desires of the soul persist in the spiritual realm?

Maybe, to flourish in the new spiritual frontier, the soul's condition must replicate the outside permeating forces, and to receive this revelation, one must have no expectations. Yes, it does seem very confusing and difficult, but simply feed your soul thoughts that will continue its ascension toward the recognition of divine nature rather than thoughts of death and decay. A minimal change will first occur. Yet, with more and more work, the spiritual will parallel the physical through the efforts put into meditational practices. Impressions from other higher worlds will soon be perceived, but to begin you must first shut the gates of the senses. The ability to decipher the ego's power to think, feel, and use will power, and incorporate this wisdom with the higher forces of nature, will only elevate your soul's knowledge!

Are those illuminated the true Extra-Terrestrials?

Food Wars

Thomas Medonis

If you control oil you control nations; if you control food you control people. –Henry Kissinger

Has a food war always existed between those who own and manage the economic agrarian upper hand of the Ukraine? It is the breadbasket of Europe with such beautiful rich soil and ranks second as the most important economic component of the former Soviet Union. On January 12, 2014, 50,000 "pro-Western" Ukrainians "descended upon Kiev's Independence Square to protest against the government of President Viktor Yanukovych… That same day, the Financial Times reported a major deal for U.S. agribusiness titan Cargill." (Corporate Interests Behind Ukraine Putsch, JP Sottile, March 16, 2014) I too must admit, I have felt the effects of this never-ending "War on Food".

In earnest, my mind has made life very difficult for the last fifteen years. In my early twenties I invested all of my savings into a large farm, refurnishing and doubling the size of a 1910 farmhouse. I was simply told that breaking off one acre from the 150 acres was all done in order to qualify to pay property taxes in rural Connecticut, and also was told, that I was able to use the farm's land to grow produce. Everything during the whole process was a secret and nothing of the sort had unfolded. Rather, a sophisticated surveillance under the guise of "Connecticut Grown" agriculture took precedent. Weddings, day-cations, and the use of media in the promotion of farms that produce large amounts of food is the "bubble" world of USDA Agriculture in New England.

Through having children and watching the USDA pay farmers to poison crops, use cutting-edge herbicides and pesticides, as well as their dependence on synthetic fertilizers, all led me to become a certified organic farmer on half an acre of my land. Consequently, last year during the 2020 pandemic I was able to donate more than eighty bags of organic greens to local food banks. But, this year, I haven't any time to pick because of the intensity of my full-time job. Hence, a lot of greens are just going to seed, which still is a very favorable natural occurrence for future organic growth. Yet, I just have become so disgusted with the USDA and American Agriculture, which should be the frontline for "Public Health". Instead, we have been brainwashed to celebrate those that drive big green tractors and receive incredible grants from "The State", all in order to experiment newly defined bio-weapons on the populace under the guise of "local agriculture".

Something tells me we are being set-up by using GMO seeds. Russia had banned GMO's, yet, Russian Agricultural production has been infiltrated by GMO's. Not to mention, Russia signed a decree prohibiting agricultural imports from the USA, EU, Australia, and Canada, all GMO powers. This move in the food war was a direct shot against those nations attempting to penetrate the agricultural markets of the Black Sea Ports. Thus, this explains the adversarial anger at Russia's acceptance of the referendum in Crimea to return to Russian jurisdiction. Without the Black Sea port, Sevastopol, the Russian Black Sea Fleet would no longer have a home, nor the ability to prohibit commerce to other Black Sea Ports.

"On December 13 Cargill announced the purchase of a stake in a Black Sea port. Cargill's port at Novorossiysk, to the east of Russia's strategically significant and historically important Crimean naval base, gives them a major entry-point to Russian markets and adds them to the list of Big Ag companies investing in ports around the Black Sea, both in Russia and Ukraine." (Corporate Interests Behind Ukraine Putsch, JP Sottile, March 16, 2014)

Russia's plans shifted from Ukraine and turned to rely on China, Turkey, Brazil, Argentina, and other South American nations for its imports into their ports, even though those nations are mostly infiltrated by GMO's. China, though, has GMO bans.

If this is a major step in the destruction of big western agribusiness companies, I applaud these efforts. From the Bloomburg.com article 2014-01-06: "China rejecting US corn as first shipment from Ukraine arrives." But, America is a sitting duck. Are we supposed to disclose the nefarious food industry and all the dark players? What will happen to our food supply? There is no one questioning what the farmer and the Bio-food industry are doing. The farmer wants perfect specimens, not naturally blemished heirlooms. Americans still want the glamorous giant Big Mac, not the grass fed beef patty unfortunately.

This is all clearly illustrated in Boston College Law Review: Volume 54, Issue 3, Article 12, 5/23/2013, <u>The Rise of the Corporate Legal Elite in the BRICS: Implications for Global Governance:</u>

"These corporations control huge human, financial, technological, and environmental resources, and engage extensively abroad where they face multiple legal challenges. As a result, it is not surprising that many of these corporations have begun to develop increasingly large and sophisticated internal legal departments. In-house counsel not only lends legitimacy to the choices corporations make as they engage in a proliferating number and variety of transactions, but it also forces corporations to think about responsible investment and business practices and provides early legal input into strategic decisions." (Boston College International & Comparative Law Review, 1157, 2013)

Among the luminaries working tirelessly and no doubt selflessly for a better, freer Ukraine are:

-Melissa Agustin, Director, International Government Affairs and Trade for Monsanto

-Brigitte Dias Ferreira, Counsel, International Affairs for John Deere

-Steven Nadherny, Director, Institutional Relations for agriculture equipment-make CNH Industrial

-Jeff Rowe, Regional Director for Dupont Pioneer

-John F. Steele, Director, International Affairs for Eli Lilly & Company

And, of course, Cargill's Van A. Yeutter. But Cargill isn't alone in their warm feelings toward Ukraine. As Reuters reported in May 2013, Monsanto, the largest seed company in the world, plans to build a $140 million 'non-GM' (genetically modified) corn seed plant in Ukraine." (Corporate Interests Behind Ukraine Putsch, JP Sottile, March 16, 2014)

Yes, modern day David vs. Goliath is real and happening right now! Grow your own food and grow cover crops to feed the soil. We have the power to boycott, we have the power to protest, and now is the most important time to do so. There is no urgency to naturally improve the soil content or to promote organic practices in the name of "public health", even as we are organic creatures of this

Earth. As long as all that rules Food is money, there will be no change.

Yes, it is true that there may never be any resolution to the genetically modified food problem as long as we seek foreign countries to become our criminal accomplices. We formed a treaty with Ukraine which was received by Congress from President Clinton on 11/10/1999. "Treaty with Ukraine on Mutual Legal Assistance in Criminal Matters" is the formal title of the treaty between the United States of America and Ukraine on Mutual Legal Assistance in Criminal Matters with Annex, signed at Kiev on July 22, 1998, and with an Exchange of Notes signed on September 30, 1999.

This food war is not yummy!

Treaty of 1213
The End of Allodial Title

Thomas Medonis

When I hear it is all white people's fault, all war is the fault of American citizen's, or the population of England is responsible for the continual expansionist conquest of independent colonies, I realize I am speaking with someone that doesn't understand that we are all sovereign.

Sovereign (n): a king, queen or other supreme ruler

Sovereign (adj): belonging to or characteristic of a sovereign or sovereign authority; royal.

Well here in America, we are all sovereign beings! Our Constitution along with the development of this experiment of America at least gives us the opportunity to prepare and administer a "Notice of Liabilities" to "The State Administrators" for their non-Constitutional conduct. And, we too, are able to recommend and receive demands for compensation for the operations of the British Accreditation Registry (BAR). To understand our enslavement under the BAR system, we must go back almost 1,000 years and rediscover two pivotal doctrines: The Treaty of 1213 and the "Unam Sanctum" of 1302. The practice of one ancient Treaty feeding into another legal agreement for complete dominion ruled under the Royal Family is simply how the "Royals" shift their power through generations.

Prior to 1066, the people of England held Allodial title to their land, as the King couldn't even think of removing land from subjects who avoided paying their tithe. William I, also known as William the Conqueror and William the Bastard, was the first Norman monarch of England. He gained sovereignty in 1066 following the death of Edward the Confessor. William invaded England leading the Norman Army over the Anglo-Saxon Forces. Thus William the Conqueror stole the Kings Title and took all the land from the natives. England would thus become bankrupt and even worse; the King administered the Law of Mortmain, which is the same as contemporary probate, in which people couldn't pass their land on to the church or anyone else without the King's permission.

The Vatican, the 108 acre plot formed in 313 A.D. after Constantine gave Pope Militades the land, did not consent with the lack of subjection by the United Kingdom's. Consequently, King John owed an incredible amount of pounds to the Vatican, and, consequently, King John refused any Vatican Representation, who Pope Innocent III had inserted. Thus, in 1208 England was placed under Papal Vatican prohibition. As King John was excommunicated he returned the title of his kingdoms of England and Ireland to the Pope as vassals, and declared submission and loyalty to the Pope and the Vatican. The control of the British Empire was now in the hands of the Roman Empire (contemporary Khazar's and International Jew's).

On October 3, 1213, the Treaty of 1213 came to fruition. King John would confirm his surrender of his kingdoms to the Pope, ruler of the Vatican, as Vicar of Christ who claimed ownership of everything. The contract of the Treaty of 1213 was between two parties, the feudal vassal's, The Baron's of England, and the Vatican. The Baron's no longer would take any subjection and took the sword to King John, in which, the King would sign the Magna Charta, sealed at Runnymede, June 15, 1215. The Vatican, however, would not comply.

Pope Innocent III declared the Magna Charta to be *"unlawful and unjust as it is base and shameful… whereby the Apostolic See is brought into contempt, the Royal Prerogative diminished, the English outraged, and the whole enterprise of the Crusade greatly imperiled."*

There are two types of people: those that prescribe to the legal standing of the Treaty of 1213 or those that deny operating under the Pope's control and are ruled under the Magna Charta. The Treaty of 1783 clearly states in the opening statement, "It having pleased the Divine Providence to dispose the hearts of the Most Serene and Most Potent Prince, George the Third, by the grace of God, King of the Great Britain, France and Ireland, Defender, of the Faith, Duke of Brunswick and Laurenberg, Arch-Treasurer and PRINCE ELECTOR OF THE HOLY ROMAN EMPIRE, & C. AND OF THE UNITED STATES OF AMERICA".

To further our subjection "Unam Sanctam" was established, control through birth certificates. If within seven days a birth certificate is not signed by the parents, the child is considered dead. Yes, our birth and death certificates are sold on Wall Street, and could be worth more than half a million dollars. Unfortunately, in our prison state we accumulate great debts and have to pay back money that is rightfully ours. Unam sanctam is a papal bull that was issued by Pope Boniface VIII on November 18th, 1302. It established dogmatic propositions on the unity of the Catholic Church, the necessity of belonging to it for eternal salvation, the position of the Pope as supreme head of the Church, and the sole duty thence arising of submission to the Pope to belong to the Church in order to reach salvation. Simply, this document made every human a subject to the Pope and the Vatican. As soon as parents sign the birth certificate, the infant belongs to the Vatican. Yes, all souls are still under the demonic control of The Vatican Order.

Yes, the Vatican has stayed prominent in world domination, but they have performed under the ever changing guises of Royalty, Companies, and Charters. Furthermore, European Kingdom's have mostly been filled with German royalty. Ha, the modern-day face associated with British royalty is in fact of German decent. In 1901, the House of Saxe-Coburg and Gotha, (a branch of the German Dynasty of Counts from the House of Wettin) succeeded the House of Hanover (the German Royal house that ruled Hanover, Great Britain), to the British monarchy with the accession of King Edward VII. These are the bloodlines of our rulers of today when it is natural for subjects to be under the rule of foreign leaders. Rulers who would trade sons and daughters with stronger kingdoms to gain dominion have ruled this world for a very long time.

The Rothschild Dynasty is no different. The leaders of the Khazarian Mafia, the force that has completely taken over and corrupted Judaism, has inserted their corporations and designs into every aspect of Earthly life. The Rothschild control of the East and West India Companies has propelled their world dominance. Actually, the Rothschild's formed and managed the Trans-Atlantic slave trade beginning in 1401, which lasted over 400 years until 1865's Civil War conclusion. However, covert slavery continues today. Wherein, it was recorded that 95% of slave owners in Confederate America were affiliates of the Khazarian Mafia. White American's were simply the foreman's, who consented to perform any evil act. The Khazarian International Jew objective is to divide the royal from the poor, the white from the black. They simply control an unsustainable system through the manipulation of thought; controlling the mind of the oppressed in order to gain great wealth from legally stealing resources. Politics is war without blood.

Prince of Academi

Thomas Medonis

How is it that former British Spy and Republican mega-donor Eric Prince had more power and influence than the actual U.S. military? The founder of the private contractor Blackwater is otherwise known as the head of a war-criminal mercenary corporate agency. Should he be locked up in a maximum security prison for the remainder of his life being guilty of foreign war crimes? RT.com reported Prince was "facing possible charges in the US for selling military services to Libya and money laundering".

Erik's father was named Edgar. 1910 U.S. Census documents disclose: Chicago Ward 33, Cook County, Illinois, Edgar's paternal grandparents were married for 4 years. The head of household was Garret Prince, age 25, shipping clerk at a paint factory. Garret immigrated in 1888 and was naturalized.

He owned a mortgaged house. He was born in Holland, as his parents, but crossed that out to write "Dutch" instead. The wife is listed as Maria, 22 years, born in Illinois of a father born in Germany and a mother born in Holland, also rewritten as "Dutch". (en.wikipedia.org)

Erik Prince's former outfit Blackwater settles lawsuit from infamous 2007 Baghdad shootout, (Garret Ellison, The Grand Rapids Press, January 8, 2012):

The Associated Press is reporting that owners of the company formerly known as Blackwater said they've settled a lawsuit brought by survivors and estates of Iraqis killed during an infamous Baghdad shooting in 2007, when Holland [Michigan] native Erik Prince was still the organization CEO. The settlement ends the lawsuit against the security contractor, now called Academi. Blackwater Security were guarding U.S. diplomats in 2007 when they opened fire in Baghdad's crowded Nisoor Square, killing 17 people, including women and children. Blackwater claimed self-defense in the incident. Prosecutor's called the attack unprovoked. Prince, a former Navy Seal,... family fortune was made in the auto parts industry. His sister, Betsy Devos, a former chairwoman of the Michigan GOP, is married to Dick DeVos, a Republican and Amway Corp. heir who unsuccessfully ran for governor in 2006.

Prince moved to Abu Dhabi in 2010, only after Blackwater provided intelligence, training, and security services to US and foreign governments as well as several multinational corporations, including Monsanto, Chevron, the Walt Disney Company, and Royal Caribbean Cruise Lines. In addition, Blackwater worked through the Defense Intelligence Agency, the Defense Threat Reduction Agency, and the US European Command. The New York Times reported that Blackwater, "created a web of more than 30 shell companies or subsidiaries in part to obtain millions of dollars in American government contracts after the security company came under intense criticism for reckless conduct in Iraq". Blackwater, consequently, was at the center of the CIA's assassination program. Prince would consequently sell Blackwater, which name had morphed into Xe Services in 2009.

    An article in The Nation: Blackwater's Black Ops, 9/15/2010 by

Jeremy Scahill reveals the clandestine intelligence service Blackwater (Total Intelligence) was hired by the multinational company Monsanto to "protect the Monsanto brand name" and become the "intel arm for Monsanto". The military contractor would ultimately have the name changed again in 2011 into Academi. Prince served as Blackwater's CEO until 2009, and he would then involve himself in a private equity firm and oversaw The Frontier Resource Group, and served as chairman of the Hong Kong listed Frontier Services Group. Any connection to The Frontier that services Connecticut's communications?

Blackwater, strangely, has changed its name numerous times and now it seems to be defined in a more academic fashion: "Academi". Why is that?

    In my experience working in education for over twenty years, while giving volunteer book talks on the most stimulating subjects to greatly accepting students and performing any task needed, my intuition tells me that the Department of Education doesn't give two craps about my efforts towards children's higher education. Education has sadly taught me that education is run for profit, not the opportunity to reach full potential for one's own individual intelligence. Data mining is the most important element of education for the government. Thus, there is an incredible amount of money to anyone that can access every innocent child's data to discover and infiltrate the next Einstein or

Tesla and turn the information into State Sponsored Technology and Initiatives.

Most recently, Prince, "Brother to former U.S. education Secretary Betsy Devos, recruited a motley crew of home-grown American operatives… to lead an initiative to infiltrate state-level Democratic Party organizations and campaigns… Ex-MI6 officer [Richard Seddon] (British Intelligence Agency) [was] recruited to head the project. Richard Seddon, also targeted moderate Republican officials those deemed as insufficiently dedicated to the hardline right-wing agenda favored by former President Donald Trump. The New York Times reported Friday. The duo were bankrolled by the longtime conservative donor and heiress to the Gore-Tex fortune. Susan Gore, and trained their operatives on a remote Wyoming ranch in areas like the "basics of espionage" and "political sabotage," according to the newspaper... Seddon and Prince placed two spies- Beau Maier, the nephew of conservative commentator Glenn Beck, and Sofia LaRocca, deep into Democratic political organizations in Wyoming, Arizona, and Colorado." (Inside The Undercover Plot To Infiltrate The Dems In The West, Zachary Petrizzo, Salon, June 26, 2021)

Yes, Erik Prince is known for founding Blackwater as a Private Military Contractor, but another fascinating connection he has is to Spectrum Health, which has close ties to the Devos family and their medical industry affiliations (Amway). The Devos family founded Amway/Alticor which operates in Russia including transactions with Alfa Bank such as buying insurance for 800 Alticor employees from Alfa Bank's insurance subsidiary. (Dailykos.com)

In Spectrum Health and Alpha bank, Trump tower servers would consequently exhibit unique only patterns: From May 4 until September 23, the Russian-based Alpha Bank repeatedly looked up the contact information for a computer server being used by the Trump Organization. The bank looked up the address to this unique Trump corporate server 2,820 times- more lookups than the Trump server received from any other source. Alfa Bank alone represents 80% of the lookups, according to these leaked internet records. In second place, with 714 internet lookups, was a company called Spectrum Health. Spectrum is a medical facility chain led by Dick Devos, the husband of Betsy Devos, who was appointed by Trump as U.S. education secretary. Together, Alfa and Spectrum accounted for 99% of the lookups by Alpha Bank. This server behavior alarmed one computer expert who had privileged access to this technical information last year. Alpha Bank maintains that the most likely explanation is that the server communication was the result of spam marketing. (CNN.Com)

Consequently, an attorney for Trump Campaign Chairman Paul Manafort was Alex Van Der Swan who is married to the daughter of the Russian oligarch who owns the Alfa banking conglomerate. Van Der Swan would also plead guilty for lying to the FBI!

What about Betsey Devos connections in education? What

personal experience did she have in education to nationally run the Department of Education? Was it all tied into some data mining operation run by her brother through military contractors?

Erik Prince said to Obama regarding the Iraq Occupation: "If you don't have the guts, just leave it to us to finish the job in Iraq". An f'ing merc trying to be our our private military AGAINST our public foreign policy decisions. (dailykos.com)

Jeremy Scahill wrote in 2004: "The Bush administration came to power with the most radical privatization agenda in U.S. history, and we see it in our schools, we see it in prisons, we see it in healthcare, we see it in local law enforcement in the United States, federal law enforcement as well. And now with the so-called war on terror and the occupation of Iraq, we've seen the most militant privatization agenda sort of unfold before our eyes."

    I type all these ideas and discoveries out to try and discover the big picture of our arrested development. In consideration that Prince and Devos ancestry goes back to the Dutch culture, maybe some answers for their actions will be found there. "Dutch" is a West Germanic language spoken by about 30 million as a first or second language. Interestingly, Dutch is also considered the closet relative to the German's and English. Dutch is said to be "roughly in between" the two powers. And, it is the Dutch House of Orange princely dynasty that is the Netherland's royal family. "Under the Dutch House of Orange, the north was to be predominant." (Britannica.com). The name "House of Orange" is derived from the old principality of Orange, the old Provence of southern France. Could Prince and Devos be descendants of the House of Orange?

Erik Prince, founder of Blackwater, claims his firm 'became a virtual extension of the CIA', taking orders from the agency. "Blackwater's work with the CIA began when we provided specialized instructors and facilities that the Agency lacked," Prince told the Daily Beast. "In the years that followed, the company became a virtual extension of the CIA because we were asked time and again to carry out dangerous missions, which the agency either could not or would not do in-house." Initially, lawmakers believed the CIA was "looking for skills and capabilities, and they had to go to outside contractors like Blackwater to make sure they could accomplish their mission," said retired Congressman Pete Hoekstra. But the relationship was in fact much closer than believed. (Blackwater was CIA's extension, founder Erik Prince admits, 14 March 2013, rt.com)

Are we currently in a "War of Civilizations"? To me, it is just incomprehensible on what has unfolded by the hands of America's most revered intelligence agency. Everything is bull crap, it is all an illusion. War, education, arts, are all bought and paid for by actors somehow connected to the military industrial complex. Has everyone in the press, politics, and on the tube been corrupted somehow or another?

Prince + Gates + Blackwater + Dutch House of Orange + Erasmus Food Labs (Netherlands) = Erasmus is a registered trademark owned by the European Union and represented by the European Commission, which is also sponsored by the Bill and Melinda Gates Foundation. Yes, Bill Gates funds the lab that "is aerosolizing deadly pathogens for deadly, pandemic causing flu['s]." Erasmus Lab in Rotterdam, Holland has long been warned of aerosolizing deadly pathogens. "Their 'gain of function' work was even halted for three years in 2015 as being too dangerous to experiment with. But the Erasmus Lab reinstated this deadly research in March 2019" (Spray It In Dutch, George Webb). The experiments the lab performs, such as aerosolizing deadly pathogens on ferrets, was paid for by Bill Gates. Investigative journalist George Webb "identified the special relations the Erasmus Lab had with the Secretary General of the United Nations through Marion Koopmans of the Erasmus Lab and Queen Maxima of the Netherlands." And, as "Henry Kissinger believes vaccinations are an instrument of foreign policy", "the daughter of Henry Kissinger's bioweapons partner is now the Queen of Netherlands." (Spray It In Dutch, George Webb)

Fouchier study reveals changes enabling airborne spread of H5N1, Robert Roos, Jun 21, 2012

"In the lengthy report, Ron Fouchier, PhD, of Erasmus Medical Center in the Netherlands and colleagues describe how they used a combination of genetic engineering and serial infection of ferrets to create a mutant H5N1 virus that can spread among ferrets without direct contact. They say their findings show that H5N1 viruses have the potential to evolve in mammals to gain airborne transmissibility, without having to mix with other flu viruses in intermediate hosts such as pigs, and thus pose a risk of launching a pandemic."

Many military and former CIA officers worked for Blackwater or related companies created to divert attention from their bad reputation and make more profit selling their nefarious services- ranging from information and intelligence to infiltration, political lobbying and paramilitary training- for other governments, banks and multinational corporations. According to Author Jeremy Scahill, business with multinationals, like Monsanto, Chevron, and financial giants such as Barclays and Deutsche Bank, are channeled through two companies owned by Erik Prince, owner of Blackwater: Total Intelligence Solutions and Terrorism Research Center. These officers and directors share Blackwater. One of them, Cofer Black, known for his brutality as one of the directors of the CIA, was the one who made contact with Monsanto in 2008 as director of Total Intelligence, entering into the contract with the company to spy on and infiltrate organizations of animal rights activists, anti-GM and other dirty activities of the biotech giant…. Scahill has copies of emails from Cofer Black after the meeting with [Monsanto Executive Kevin] Wilson, where he explains to other former CIA agents, using their Blackwater e-mails, that the discussion with Wilson was that Total Intelligence had become "Monsanto's intelligence arm," spying on activists and other actions, including "our people to legally integrate these groups." Monsanto paid Total Intelligence (Blackwater) $127,000 in 2008 and $105,000 in 2009. No wonder that a company engaged in the "science of death" as Monsanto, which has been dedicated from the outset to produce toxic poisons spilling from Agent Orange to PCBs (polychlorinated biphenyls), pesticides, hormones and genetically modified seeds, is associated with another company of thugs… Via Campesina reported the purchase of 500,000 shares of Monsanto, for more than $23 million by the Bill and Melinda Gates Foundation. (Machines of War: Blackwater, Monsanto, and Bill Gates, femalefaust.blogspot.com, Oct 16, 2010)

www.ingramcontent.com/pod-product-compliance
Lightning Source LLC
Chambersburg PA
CBHW070419220526
45466CB00004B/1468